INSPIRED TRAVELLER'S GUIDE
LITERARY PLACES

INSPIRED TRAVELLER'S GUIDE

LITERARY PLACES

SARAH BAXTER

ILLUSTRATIONS BY
AMY GRIMES

WHITE LION
PUBLISHING

Brimming with creative inspiration, how-to projects and useful information to enrich your everyday life, Quarto Knows is a favourite destination for those pursuing their interests and passions. Visit our site and dig deeper with our books into your area of interest: Quarto Creates, Quarto Cooks, Quarto Homes, Quarto Lives, Quarto Drives, Quarto Explores, Quarto Gifts, or Quarto Kids.

First published in 2019 by White Lion Publishing,
an imprint of The Quarto Group.
The Old Brewery, 6 Blundell Street,
London, N7 9BH,
United Kingdom
T (0)20 7700 6700
www.QuartoKnows.com

A catalogue record for this book is available from the British Library.

ISBN 978 1 78131 810 2
Ebook ISBN 978 1 78131 811 9

10 9 8 7 6 5 4 3 2 1

Design by Paileen Currie

Printed in China

CONTENTS

INTRODUCTION

TURN OVER the page. What – or where – do you see? Perhaps you see city streets or verdant fields, vast mountain ranges or dark, haunted forests, stinking slums or golden temples. A multitude of worlds written into being. Palaces of words, landscapes of letters, towns built of sentences. Whole societies or galaxies constructed from carefully laid conjunctions, stocky nouns, playful verbs; from swirls and curlicues of ink.

Writers build places. Sometimes they conjure make-believe realms, unfettered by rules of sense or science. But sometimes they evoke real ones – destinations you can find on a map. And sometimes they manage to make those real places feel more real than any photo ever could. They render locations large in mere ink, perfectly capturing their sights, sounds, smells and essence, turning a previously blank sheet into a teleporter for the reader's imagination.

Truly great writers recreate not only locations but also eras and histories. Indeed, via some classic works of literature, a reader can travel both around the world and seemingly back in time: to the plains of medieval Spain, to the squalor of Victorian London, to the horror of apartheid-divided South Africa. The very best writers bring not only the physicality of these destinations to life but also their layers; their nooks and crannies, their politics and their position in the world. In this way, these destinations can come alive for people living in different countries, on different continents, even in different centuries. Not everyone is able to travel. And no one – not yet – can travel in time. So by reading great books anyone, of any nation, is able to 'journey' to a totally other period and place.

In this book we have focused on just 25 great literary places – a much-deliberated shortlist of intriguing locations that have featured, if not starred, in some of the best novels ever penned. With the help of beautiful illustrations, this armchair guide hopes to convey you to these varied spots, spread all over the globe. Many of them you may know, some you may not. But, with luck, every chapter will transport you, for a moment at least, to somewhere else entirely – be it the politically and seismically shaken Chilean countryside (page 140), the beer-sticky and insalubrious bars of 1900s Dublin (page 16) or the languid backwaters of southern India, where death and incest lurk behind every swaying palm (page 92).

In many cases the destinations collected here aren't just passive backdrops to the tragedies, romances and adventures that unfold within them. These destinations become characters in their own right, rising up from behind the scenes to take centre stage; they have agency, influencing plot, action, emotions and outcomes.

For instance, consider the North York Moors of Emily Brontë's *Wuthering Heights* (page 78). This heather-fuzzed, wind-whipped wilderness, where the literary Brontë family lived, played and wrote, may as well be listed in the novel's dramatis personae. The moors feel as corporeal, untameable, moody and brooding as *Wuthering Heights'* antihero Heathcliff himself. It's utterly impossible to imagine this strange 19th-century Gothic romance – so fierce and full of passion – set anywhere else on the planet. The author and her masterpiece are both inseparable from this soil.

Likewise, Holden Caulfield's iconic episode of teenage angst, as portrayed in J.D. Salinger's *The Catcher in the Rye* (page 110), wouldn't have quite the impact if it wasn't set on the hustling, bustling, grim-and-glamorous avenues of late-1940s Manhattan. Salinger captures the mid-century metropolis, with its pimps and phonies and elusive ducks, at a defining moment – a time when New York was both dealing with the dark aftermath of the Second World War and booming on the world scene. The city's external chaos and confusion mirror the inner turmoil in the young protagonist's mind.

In some cases the words, the place, the culture and the events are so intertwined and richly rendered in a novel that reading it is akin to absorbing the best sort of history lesson, without even noticing. The Cairo Trilogy by Naguib Mahfouz (page 82) not only describes the specific geography of the Egyptian capital's most atmospheric neighbourhood, it weaves in myriad strands – from cookery to religion, architecture to 20th-century politics – to create an elaborate carpet of a book. You can be enthralled by the narrative of the al-Jawad family, as you might be by any such saga, but you'll also come away better educated about Islam and about what has made Egypt the country it is today.

There are many, many more literary locations that could have been included here – places so brilliantly evoked in books that you can almost smell the dirt, dust or blood on their pages. For example, we could have taken a murderous cruise down the Nile with crime queen Agatha Christie; we might have explored Istanbul through the Nobel Prize-winning pages of local-born Orhan Pamuk; or we could have followed the sinister Dracula trail laid in Romania by Bram Stoker. Sadly, the pages of this modest book are limited to covering only 25 others. But maybe by reading a little about this handful of wonderful written worlds you might feel inspired to either read the original tomes or to continue your literary travels by seeking out more globe-trotting works. Who knows? You might even feel moved to travel to some of the real-life locations and try encapsulating them on paper yourself ...

Which?	*Les Misérables* by Victor Hugo (1862)
What?	French City of Light, squalor, revolution, *égalité* and Enlightenment

PARIS

DO YOU hear the people sing? The angry men, demanding to be heard? Once, before these elegant boulevards ploughed through the congested slums, this city screamed with revolution; tight-packed, disease-festered alleys clogged with barricades and voices yearning for *liberté, égalité, fraternité*. Now, the avenues are wide, bright, brimming with bonhomie; the noise is of coffee cups chinking on enamel tabletops, breezes rattling the neat plane trees. These streets are elegance and *amour* incarnate. But once they flowed with blood ...

By the 1850s – when Victor Hugo was writing *Les Misérables* – Paris was quite literally the City of Light. Around 15,000 newly installed gaslights illuminated the French capital. Night-times became safer; citizens were drawn to the streets at all hours – a pavement culture that endures today. But just a few decades before, when *Les Misérables* is set, the city was a far darker place. Paris may have birthed the 18th-century's intellectual Enlightenment but, for the impoverished majority, it was still rife with inequality and despair. As Hugo once wrote, 'He who contemplates the depths of Paris is seized with vertigo. Nothing is more fantastic. Nothing is more tragic. Nothing is more sublime.'

Les Misérables contains all of those qualities. One of the longest novels ever written, it charts the travails of Jean Valjean, beginning in 1815, as he's paroled after nearly two decades in prison for stealing a loaf of bread, and finishing in the aftermath of the 1832 Paris Uprising, when Valjean finds redemption on his deathbed.

During this period, the city was still the 'old Paris' that Hugo loved, a labyrinth of narrow, intertwining streets, courtyards and crannies where characters could slip easily into the shadows. However, the city was also overcrowded, unhealthy and increasingly disillusioned: despite the world-upending 1789 Revolution, France seemed to be sinking back into aristocratic ways. Hence the Uprising. On 5 June 1832 around 3,000 Republican insurgents briefly controlled eastern and central Paris, an area spanning from the Châtelet to the Île de la Cité and Faubourg Saint-Antoine; barricades rose in the streets off rue Saint-Denis. But by 6 June the reinforced National Guard had stamped out the rebellion. Around 800 people were killed or wounded.

Hugo himself witnessed the riots. He was writing in the Tuileries Garden when he heard gunshots from the direction of Les Halles, the traditional market area with its warren of alleys (now replaced by a shopping mall). He followed the noise north, but was forced to shelter in passage du Saumon (now passage Ben-Aïad – closed to the public), while bullets whizzed past.

The city has changed immeasurably since. Between 1853 and 1870, urban planner Baron Haussmann razed much of the medieval city, replacing its ancient chaos with modern order: broad, straight boulevards, open intersections, public parks, harmonious terraces of mansard-roofed mansions. Avenues were made wide enough for carriages; they were also made too wide for effective barricades. The result was a city more homogenous, more hygienic, arguably more handsome but stripped of centuries of history.

Haussmann has certainly made it more difficult to follow in the footsteps of Valjean, his ward Cosette, her suitor Marius and the rest of Hugo's revolutionaries, vagabonds, gendarmes and whores. But echoes of his Paris remain. Most evocative is the Marais (the marsh), where there are more intact medieval buildings than anywhere else in the city. This neighbourhood on the Right Bank of the Seine survived Haussmannisation; it's still a maze of tight-knit cobbled lanes, easy to get lost in, and now jam-packed with bookshops, boutiques, bars and cafés. It's in the Marais that you'll find the Places des Vosges, a perfect, tree-lined square framed by arcaded 17th-century houses, one of which is Hugo's former home (now a museum). At the heart of the Marais is the baroque Jesuit church of Saint-Paul-Saint-Louis, where Marius and Cosette are

in microcosm – is assembled in safe, neutral Switzerland to debate culture and philosophy. But as the patients in the sanatorium seek a cure, Europe beyond is sick. The novel begins in the first decade of the 20th century, the continent on the brink of war. When Castorp eventually leaves his alpine bubble seven years later, it's for the trenches. The final pages leave him limping across the mud, bombs falling, alive but with 'prospects poor'.

The hellish trenches are certainly a far cry from Mann's bewitched Swiss valley setting, where 'the towering statues of snow-clad Alps' can awaken 'feelings of the sublime and holy'. The high mountain town of Davos, in the canton of Graubünden, is now best known for hosting the annual World Economic Forum. But, from the mid-19th century, it was a popular spot for the sick. Many doctors believed the town's alpine air and microclimate were ideal for combatting illnesses, in particular tuberculosis. Some two dozen sanatoriums opened here, and patients spent hours sitting on terraces, wrapped in blankets, soaking up the sunshine; they'd take constitutionals, drink creamy milk and wine and breathe in deep lungfuls of the crisp, clear air.

Though not a precise version of Thomas Mann's fictional Berghof, the Schatzalp is a good approximation. Floating high on the mountainside above Davos, it opened as a luxury clinic in 1900. The funicular train, which conveyed patients up in minutes, is still the only way to get there, other than on foot. Being higher up the valley, the Schatzalp receives more sunshine than the town below, and the sanatorium was built facing south to optimise exposure to natural light. Its long, wind-sheltered verandas allowed patients to recline on deckchairs in the sun, enjoying the very best views.

The Schatzalp was converted into a hotel in the 1950s, when innovations such as penicillin killed the sanatorium industry. It has retained much belle époque charm, from its stained glass and painted peacocks to the hundred-year-old plumbing. There are also nods to its medicinal history – the lightbox panels above the bar reveal that this used to be the X-ray room.

A Thomas Mann Way walking path, dotted with quotations from *The Magic Mountain*, now connects the Schatzalp to Davos, via the Waldhotel – formerly the Woodland Sanatorium. This is where Katia Mann was recuperating from a lung complaint when her husband, Thomas, came to visit in spring 1912 and decided that this could be the setting for a good story ...

Which?	*Northanger Abbey* & *Persuasion* by Jane Austen (1818)
What?	Splendid English city, setting for a send-up of Georgian high society

BATH

THE CRESCENT'S honeyed stone glows in the afternoon sunlight, a radiant architectural swoosh between the neat green lawn and cloudless blue sky. A long procession of Ionic columns and sash windows sweeps away in perfect symmetry, while the footsteps of the slowly strolling curious – faces up-turned, mouths agape – slap on worn-smooth slabs. Such splendour! But look behind the flawless facade and this elegant terrace tells a different story. Round the other side it's an untidy irregularity of annexes and add-ons. A Queen Anne front, a Mary-Anne back. A public face concealing darker truths ...

'Oh! Who can ever be tired of Bath?' Who indeed. In *Northanger Abbey*, Jane Austen's playful satire on the Gothic novel, heroine Catherine Morland speaks of the allure of the Somerset city in the early 19th century – an allure that continues to this day. In England, there is nowhere else quite like it; nowhere as perfectly, homogeneously preserved. To walk along its sweeping crescents and golden streets now is almost to step straight back into Austen's pages, minus the bonnets and breeches.

Bath nestles within a loop of the River Avon, on the southern edge of the rolling-green Cotswold Hills. The city owes its situation and success to its hot springs, unique in Britain, and first developed by the Romans who built an elaborate bathing complex here, which they called *Aquae Sulis*. Though the Roman temple fell into disuse, and was eventually forgotten – until its rediscovery in 1775 – these healing waters continued to be sought after. From the 17th century, following a succession of royal visits, Bath became the *resort du jour*,

ΑΡΙΣΤΟΝΜΕΝΥΔΩΡ

THE
PUMP
ROOM

with society's finest coming here for 'the season' to bathe, drink, see, be seen, gossip and matchmake. Befitting its status, the city was given a stylish Georgian facelift, with father-and-son architects John Wood the Elder (1704–1754) and Younger (1728–1782) remodelling the city, using the local golden limestone. Between them they designed many splendid streets and edifices: Queen Square, the perfect Palladian ring of The Circus, the grand Assembly Rooms, the Royal Crescent's curve of 30 classical townhouses. By the time Jane Austen moved to Bath in 1801, living here until 1806, it was the most coherent and majestic of cityscapes, even if its fashionability was beginning to wane.

Austen herself wasn't especially enamoured with Bath. She was a creature of the countryside and found the city's superficiality and ostentation overbearing. But it provided rich creative pickings. An entire city obsessed with manners and class was a useful backdrop for her brand of quick-witted, acerbic social commentary. Two of her novels, *Northanger Abbey* and *Persuasion,* which were first published in one volume in 1818 shortly after Austen's death, are partly set in the city. They offer not only a picture of Bath, but of English high society during the Regency era.

Balls and parties were an integral part of fashionable life. Jane herself, as well as *Northanger*'s Catherine and *Persuasion*'s Anne Elliot, attended gatherings at Bath's Assembly Rooms, opened in 1771, where four public rooms – the Octagon, Ball Room, Card Room and Tea Room – allowed for all sorts of socialising. The huge 18th-century crystal chandeliers, under which Austen's envoys would have danced and whispered, still dazzle from the soaring ceilings; now the building also houses the Fashion Museum, where you can try on Georgian hats and dresses.

The Pump Room was another must in Austen's time. The beau monde would visit this colonnaded building by Bath Abbey to take either the curative waters or afternoon tea, to listen to the orchestra and to 'parade up and down for an hour, looking at everybody and speaking to no one'. It was during preparatory investigations into the construction of the Pump Room that the remains of the Roman complex were rediscovered. Today, part of this grand meeting place is the excellent Roman Baths museum, where you can descend into an underbelly of ancient pools, temples and hypocausts. However, in the Pump Room's fine main hall, you can still eat cake and finger sandwiches, and you can still sip the medicinal, if foul-tasting, mineral waters from the King's Spring.

One of the real beauties of Bath is that so much is so unchanged. And not just the landmark buildings but the layout of the streets themselves. For instance, Austen has her players shopping on lively Milsom Street, still one of the city's premier retail rows; look up above the modern shop fronts to the tops of the buildings and you're transported back in time. Austen's characters also promenade Great Pulteney Street – still the city's most impressive Georgian avenue – and take carriages up to the 'lofty, dignified situation' of Camden Place, a little-touristed terrace affording excellent views if you can bear the stiff walk up.

Northanger's Catherine hastens to the Royal Crescent 'to breathe the fresh air of better company' (today many go to visit No. 1, now a museum furnished in 18th-century style). Meanwhile, at the close of *Persuasion*, Anne and her Captain Wentworth reconcile along the tree-lined Gravel Walk, which still connects the Royal Crescent with Queen Square.

Bath has become synonymous with Austen. Despite the destructive Bath Blitz of April 1942 and the so-called 'Sack of Bath' in the 1960s, when ill-thought urban development saw some heritage lost, the Georgian spirit of the city remains. It's easy to envisage the streets filled with ladies in their white gloves and empire-line dresses, and gents in their tailcoats and cravats. Come during the annual autumn Jane Austen Festival and you don't even need to imagine, as Catherine Morland and Anne Elliot-alikes really do flood the streets, their slippers and gauze gowns grazing the cobbles – Austen's creations come to life.

Which?	*Oliver Twist* by Charles Dickens (1839)
What?	Den of grime and crime, where the tale of an orphan augured British social reform

LONDON

THIS CITY is a still labyrinth; a confusion of hither-thither streets, grunge and clamour, too many people. The pea-soup fog and miasma of desperation have largely lifted, but many a corner still conjures up the past. When the constant din was of horse-clatter, cab-rattle and peddler-patter. When the streets were packed with prostitutes, pickpockets, fraudsters, gangsters, ragamuffins and the piteously poor. When crime was so rife, your handkerchief might be pinched at one end of an alley and hawked back to you at the other. A city writ larger than life; wondrous and wretched in equal measure ...

All of London is laced with Charles Dickens. It seems there's barely a pub he didn't drink in, a street he didn't stroll. Moreover, he painted so strong a portrait of the UK capital at the beginning of the Victorian age that, while the city has existed for over 2,000 years, 'Dickens' London' is the incarnation that most vividly endures.

Charles Dickens was born in Portsmouth in 1812. When his father was sent to debtors' prison in 1822, young Charles was sent to work at a boot-polish warehouse on Hungerford Steps (now the site of London's Charing Cross Station). The experience left a lasting impression, fermenting his views on socioeconomic reform and the heinous labour conditions borne by the underclasses – a situation that got worse when the 1834 Poor Law Amendment Act stopped virtually all financial aid to the poverty stricken. At this time, London was the world's biggest city, an imperial and industrial powerhouse. But it was seething with destitution and class division.

Into this arena came *Oliver Twist*. Dickens' second major work, the novel pulled no punches, describing with ruthless satire the

CHARTERHOUSE STREET

LIVERPOOL
STREET
STATION

THE OLD
BAILEY

ST PAUL'S
CATHEDRAL

BANK

MONUMENT

TOWER OF
LONDON

LONDON
BRIDGE

levels of crime and depravity rife in the capital. For fictional Oliver – like so many real Londoners – the city's streets were full of 'foul and frowsy dens, where vice is closely packed and lacks the room to turn'. Via the tale of the workhouse orphan who ends up embroiled with Fagin's gang, Dickens shone a gaslight on the horrors of life on the margins in mid-19th-century Britain.

Dickens saw the sordidness first-hand. In 1837 he moved to 48 Doughty Street in Holborn, where he wrote *Oliver Twist*. Dickens was a great wanderer, and the streets he paced seeped into his pages. And the areas around his former home, which is now the Charles Dickens Museum, still whisper of the past.

A little east of Doughty Street lie the alleyways of Clerkenwell. In the early 19th century this was one of London's most squalid, crime-ridden neighbourhoods, teeming with thieves and hoodlums. In the 1860s an improvement project cleared the 'rookeries' (slums) and Clerkenwell was transformed. However, you can still walk across Clerkenwell Green, where Oliver watches in horror as the Artful Dodger pickpockets Mr Brownlow. And you can still, like Dodger, 'scud at a rapid pace' along the nearby alleys towards Saffron Hill. Named for the spice that was grown here in the Middle Ages (to mask the taste of rotten meat), in Dickens' time this was the site of an infamous rookery beside the sewage-stinking Fleet Ditch. Saffron Hill is now a nondescript sinew of offices and apartments but there's atmosphere within The One Tun pub. Founded in 1759, but rebuilt in 1875, it's reputed to be the basis for Dickens' Three Cripples, the favourite haunt of murderous villain Bill Sikes. Field Lane, the location of Fagin's lair, was demolished in the clear-up, but probably stood a little south of the pub, near where Saffron Hill meets Charterhouse Street.

Continue further south and you end up before Lady Justice and the Old Bailey, the country's Central Criminal Court. Part of it is built on the site of Newgate Prison, a gaol since the 12th century, whose 'dreadful walls ... have hidden so much misery'. Dickens witnessed a public execution here, and sent Fagin to its gallows – in *Oliver Twist*, the bad 'uns get their comeuppance, the good live happily ever after. For Victorian London's real working classes, life was seldom so fair. But through his words, Dickens ensured they were not ignored.

Which?	*Cannery Row* by John Steinbeck (1945)
What?	Ocean-side California street where life at its most colourful ebbs and flows

MONTEREY

IN THE early, pearly morning, The Row begins to wake. Gulls start their vigils on corrugated-iron rooftops, waiting for trash to become lunch; sea lions bark like hunting dogs over the heave of the ocean. People stir, feet flip-flapping along the tidy sidewalk. A new cast of human characters thrives here now: trinket-shop keepers, aquarium cleaners, tourist dealers. The whole street spruced up for a huge new shoal: visitors in their millions. But back in the day, when the factories were grinding, empty lots lay under mallow weeds and the air reeked of rotten fish, it was a different troupe – vagrants, prostitutes, artists, idlers – who frequented this industrious neighbourhood by the sea. Like a human rock pool, Cannery Row was flow and vitality, colour and oddity, a discrete ecosystem of humanity striving to stay afloat ...

Cannery Row, a waterfront avenue in Monterey, California, is one of the most famous streets in America. John Steinbeck was born in Salinas, a little northeast of Monterey, in 1902, and set many of his works in this area of central California where the Coast Ranges and rich agricultural valleys – the 'salad bowl of the States' – meet the Pacific Ocean.

By 1930, Steinbeck had moved to Pacific Grove, close to Ocean View Avenue, aka Cannery Row. It was a street lined with noisy, stinking sardine canneries that processed the spoils of the nutrient-rich water offshore – for a time, one of the most productive fishing grounds in the world. The stock seemed inexhaustible, and huge purse-seiners with nets a quarter-mile long ravaged the ocean. This kept workers working during the Great Depression and fed needy

mouths during the Second World War. But by the mid-1950s, the sardine supply ran dry. The industry collapsed; the last cannery closed in 1973.

Published in 1945, but set in an indeterminate period before that, Steinbeck's eponymous novel remembers The Row with fond sentiment. There are no Nazis in these pages. Indeed, Steinbeck himself called *Cannery Row* a 'kind of nostalgic thing', penned for a group of soldiers who asked him to 'write something funny that isn't about the war'.

The resulting book is like a series of vivid portraits, showing life on The Row in all its odoriferous, eccentric, enterprising glory. The plot, such as it is, follows the exploits of Mack and the boys, a band of resourceful bums who doss in an empty fishmeal shack. Mack decides they should do something nice for Doc, the intellectual proprietor of a biological supplies lab, whom everybody loves – and who Steinbeck based on his close friend, marine biologist and philosopher Ed Ricketts.

The resulting party ends in disaster – but that's not really the point. The novel is less about action than atmosphere. And it oozes affection for this ramshackle street and those living upon it. These folks may be a motley crew of down-and-outs and chancers, but they are mostly heart-of-gold.

Today's Cannery Row – as Ocean View Avenue was officially renamed in 1958 – bears little resemblance to Steinbeck's. For him, the street was 'a poem, a stink, a grating noise, a quality of light, a tone, a habit, a nostalgia, a dream'. The light is still right – the golden California sun still flickers off the water and down the wharf, bathing the honking sea lions and the wooden piers. But it's all a lot tidier now. The stench has gone, and the defunct factories have been given new leases of life as fish restaurants, gift shops, candy stores and antiques boutiques.

In Steinbeck Plaza, halfway along The Row, a statue depicts some of the area's characters, including Steinbeck, Ed Ricketts and local brothel madam Flora Woods, who gave food to the poor during the Depression and provided inspiration for the novel's Dora Flood. Just off The Row near here are three Cannery Row Workers' Cabins, now little museums that give a glimpse of living conditions during the district's sardine fishing heyday.

Further along the street sit real-life buildings that Steinbeck weaved in. There's Wing Chong Market, which became Lee Chong's

Heavenly Flower Grocery where you could buy everything from silk kimonos to Old Tennis Shoes whiskey. There's also Austino's Patisserie, once the site of a bordello on which Steinbeck based his La Ida Café.

At No. 800 is Ed Ricketts' clapboard Pacific Biological Laboratories – inspiration for 'Doc's Lab'. Like Doc, Ricketts preserved marine specimens here, which were bought by institutions across the country. A public walkway leads to the rear where you can still see the concrete tanks where Ricketts kept his samples; the ocean beyond is now the Edward F. Ricketts State Marine Conservation Area. Ricketts was an intellectual with diverse interests and his lab became a gathering place for artists, musicians and writers. These days the building is mostly closed, though free public tours run once a month.

Even if Doc's isn't open, you can see plenty of marine specimens on the site of the former Hovden Cannery. Since 1984, this has been home to the Monterey Bay Aquarium, a groundbreaking, not-for-profit facility dedicated to marine conservation and education, with a focus on the wildlife of Monterey Bay. The aquarium is home to some 550-plus species, from sea turtles to huge shoals of glittering sardines. Millions of paying visitors come each year. So while times may have changed, it's still fish that bring the dollars to Cannery Row.

MISSISSIPPI RIVER

SOMETIMES THIS river seems wide as an ocean. A great blue-grey expanse, slipping ever southwards from glacial lakes and tallgrass prairie to the sultry subtropics. It makes a massive, meandering journey, but is a place for simple pleasures; where you can float away from your troubles. It's a place for lazing back, trailing a toe in the flow, and listening to the somnolent trickle. For eating mushmelon and corn dodgers, talking aimless flapdoodle. For gliding to the hum of mosquitoes. For gazing at a sky a-flicker with stars. The ancient river: an invitation to drift, an opportunity to escape ...

Ol' Man River, Big Muddy, Father of Waters. The Mississippi, a leviathan of many names, flows through the heart of America. It once served as the country's western border, and has long been key for trade and transportation. During the American Civil War (1861–1865), the river's capture by Union forces signalled a turn towards victory. In short, the Mississippi looms large in America's history, culture and consciousness. And it's central to Mark Twain's *Adventures of Huckleberry Finn*.

Samuel Langhorne Clemens – pen name Mark Twain – was born in Florida, Missouri, in 1835 but moved to nearby Hannibal, on the Mississippi's west bank, in 1839. He was raised in antebellum America, a time of growth and expansion, thriving plantations and goods-laden steamboats; as a young man, Twain even worked as a riverboat pilot, gaining intimacy with the Mississippi's many twists, turns and eddies.

This was also a time of slavery. Unlike Illinois, across the river, Missouri, was not a free state; by the mid-19th century, a quarter of

Hannibal County's population were slaves. While *Adventures of Huckleberry Finn* was published two decades after the 1865 Thirteenth Amendment abolished slavery, the novel is set in the 1840s. And Twain's novel – at first glance, a simple boys' own adventure – is a blistering examination of American attitudes to race at the time.

The novel follows the exploits of teenage vagabond Huck Finn and Jim, a black adult slave. Both live in the Missouri town of St Petersburg and both want to escape incarceration. Huck is running from his abusive, alcoholic Pap and the constraints of 'sivilized' society – the hand-washin', meal times and starchy britches that have been inflicted on him. Jim is fleeing slavery. So the pair strike out together, intending to raft to the free state of Illinois. Their drifting comes at a cost – they lose their raft, witness a massacre, encounter burglars and murderers. But despite all this, the wandering river provides the ultimate prize: freedom. Unlike life ashore, it's not 'cramped up and smothery'. Once they're sliding down the Mississippi, it's as if they exist beyond society's normal rules. On the water, a white boy and a black man can float together, talking as equals.

Academics argue over Twain's stance on race. Some see the novel as a scathing attack on prejudice; others condemn its repeated use of the word 'nigger' and feel it stereotypes black people. But it remains one of the most important works of American literature, as well as a rich evocation of the mid-19th-century Midwest.

To get a taste of Twain's Americana, head to his one-time hometown of Hannibal, on which fictional St Petersburg is heavily based. The heart of the riverside town remains largely intact, its gridded historic centre lined with old-fashioned drugstores and taverns, as well as the old Clemens' house, now the Mark Twain Boyhood Home & Museum. You can also soak up the scenery that inspired Huck's adventures – the sandbanks, the old mansions, the lazy river views – and board a replica paddle steamer for a journey on the Mississippi.

A few miles south of Hannibal is Jackson's Island, where Huck and Jim meet up and forge one of the most monumental friendships in American literature – a mixed-race mate-ship in an era when this was rare indeed. The narrow, wooded island is still uninhabited, aside from the muskrats, turtles and beavers. And it's still an ideal spot to play, hide, lark, tumble and watch the timeless river glide by.

Which?	*To Kill a Mockingbird* by Harper Lee (1960)
What?	Deep South US town that inspired a simple tale of racial heroism

MONROEVILLE

NO ONE'S in a hurry in this tired old town. Maybe it's the heat – the Alabama summer is stultifying, sticky as molasses. It would be swell to swing on a porch all afternoon with an icy Coca-Cola. But this bench under the main square's live oaks and magnolias will do just fine. Folk pass by, strolling between the Christian bookshop, the thrift store and the fine old County Courthouse, its white dome dazzling under the sun. No case has been tried here for decades; indeed, its most famous case wasn't tried here at all. But it remains a potent symbol of justice all the same ...

Harper Lee's classic, *To Kill a Mockingbird*, delivered the right message in the right tone at the right moment. A simple tale of prejudice, unjustness and morality, it was published in 1960, just as the American South faced its biggest social shift since the Civil War. The equality movement was gaining momentum; deeply entrenched attitudes to race and class were being challenged. Alabama saw some of the highest-profile acts. It was in Montgomery in 1955 that Rosa Parks refused to surrender her bus seat to a white passenger. In 1956, anti-integration riots erupted when Autherine Lucy and Polly Myers became the first African-American students to be admitted to the state's university.

Though set in 1930s Alabama, during the Great Depression, *To Kill a Mockingbird* matched the mood of the sixties, and gave voice to the fears and frustrations of this transitional period. It showed the country it needed a conscience and offered an unimpeachable hero: Atticus Finch – single parent, lawyer, 'the bravest man who ever lived'. Atticus, the father of child narrator Scout, defends Tom